Vocabulary Skills

Contents

Vocabulary Skills, Grade 3, Introduction

One of the most basic elements of reading comprehension is understanding the meaning of words. However, students may not realize that they do not necessarily need to know the meaning of every word in a selection in order to understand what they are reading. They may be surprised to find that through reading, they can actually increase their knowledge of word meaning. The more words students know, the more they will be able to read, and conversely, the more they read, the more words they will know.

Students can use several strategies to help them determine the meaning of unfamiliar words they encounter while reading:
• using context clues
• analyzing prefixes, suffixes, and root words
• looking up unfamiliar words in the dictionary

Vocabulary Skills is designed to help students practice these strategies in order to incorporate them seamlessly into their approach to reading. New vocabulary words are introduced within the context of high-interest readings. Students can use these context clues to determine the meaning of unfamiliar words. Activities are designed to reinforce the use of all word meaning strategies.

By increasing their word power, students will also increase their scores on standardized tests.

Organization
The book is organized into five units, with five lessons in each unit. In Units 1–4, each lesson consists of a high-interest reading rich in context so that students can determine the meaning of the vocabulary words based on the context of the reading. Each lesson includes vocabulary activities and most contain a dictionary activity. The vocabulary activities include
• analogies,
• antonyms,
• base words,
• classifying,
• compound words,
• crossword puzzles,
• multiple meanings,
• synonyms,
• word groups,
• word puzzles, and
• word webs.

The dictionary skills include
• alphabetical order,
• guide words,
• syllabication, and
• pronunciation.

Each lesson provides a review of the vocabulary words, once again in a context-based approach, and gives students the chance to practice using the vocabulary words in their own original writing.

Unit 5 focuses on word analysis, with lessons dealing specifically with prefixes, suffixes, Greek and Latin roots, homophones, and words from other languages. The book concludes with a fun section so that students have the opportunity to play games with words.

Assessments
Vocabulary Skills uses two kinds of assessments:
• Two overall assessments located at the front of the book cover the new vocabulary words. One of these can be given as a pretest to gauge students' knowledge of the vocabulary. Later in the year, the other test can be administered to determine students' understanding, progress, and achievement.
• Each unit also has an assessment. These unit assessments can be administered at any time during the unit as a pretest, review, or posttest.

Vocabulary List
On page 3 is a list of all the vocabulary words contained in Units 1–4. You may want to distribute it to students so they will be able to incorporate the words into their writing for other assignments.

Correlation to Standards
The National Council of Teachers of English has stated in the "Standards for the English Language Arts" the following: "Students apply a wide range of strategies to comprehend, interpret, evaluate, and appreciate texts. They draw on their prior experience, their interaction with other readers and writers, their knowledge of word meaning and of other texts, their word identification strategies, and their understanding of textual features (e.g., sound-letter correspondence, sentence structure, context, graphics)." *Vocabulary Skills* helps students achieve this goal by providing strategies for students to comprehend what they read, increase their knowledge of word meaning, and expand their use of context clues.

Dictionaries and Other Reference Books
Students striving to increase their vocabulary benefit greatly from having access to dictionaries, thesauruses, and other books dealing with word meanings and origins. These resources should be readily available to students at all times.

Vocabulary List

airport (11)
amazed (14)
ankle (4)
astonished (13)

baseball (11)
bent (14)
bored (1)
brave (1)
breeds (3)
burglar (8)
business (10)

canoe (15)
cautious (1)
character (9)
cheerful (18)
childhood (13)
classroom (11)
cleanse (5)
clues (8)
compass (15)
consumed (19)
content (14)
continue (18)
crafty (6)
crooked (18)
cycles (20)

damage (4)
delicious (19)
depths (16)
discovered (6)
disguised (6)
dove (14)
dull (1)

ecosystem (20)
electricity (17)
embraced (6)
emperor (7)
enjoy (3)
equal (3)
errors (9)
exciting (10)
exercise (12)

familiar (19)
felines (5)
flashlight (17)
foolish (8)
frightened (17)
frigid (12)
frisky (5)
fuel (20)

gift (7)
grumpy (15)

hallway (11)
haste (8)
homesick (13)
homework (11)

imagination (10)

lead (2)
leash (2)
legends (9)
lightning (17)

make-believe (10)
massive (3)
molten (16)

nutrients (20)

orbits (16)
outdoorsmen (15)

palm (14)
panic (18)
peaceful (5)
perspiration (12)
petite (3)
poncho (15)
pursuing (4)

rare (7)
received (7)
reminded (13)

scratch (2)
seacoast (13)
shallow (18)
silk (7)
smoldered (20)
sneaking (6)
solve (8)
sore (4)
supermarket (12)
surface (16)
swift (9)

tart (19)
tear (2)
thud (4)
thunder (17)
timid (1)
tramp (12)

unbelievable (5)
universe (16)
usually (9)

varieties (19)
various (10)

wound (2)

Note: The numbers in parentheses refer to the lessons where the vocabulary words are taught.

Overall Assessment 1

Darken the letter of the word that fits best in the sentence.

1. Pam _____ her mother with her arms before she left.
   - Ⓐ sneaking
   - Ⓑ crafty
   - Ⓒ embraced
   - Ⓓ disguised

2. Dad _____ that his wallet was missing after we left the house.
   - Ⓐ received
   - Ⓑ discovered
   - Ⓒ astonished
   - Ⓓ frightened

3. Mr. Wong likes to buy _____ books that are not well known.
   - Ⓐ silk
   - Ⓑ crooked
   - Ⓒ rare
   - Ⓓ delicious

4. Mother hid the toy train because she did not want Dan to see his _____.
   - Ⓐ gift
   - Ⓑ cake
   - Ⓒ candle
   - Ⓓ card

5. Miss Rogers showed the class how to _____ the math problem.
   - Ⓐ damage
   - Ⓑ lead
   - Ⓒ poncho
   - Ⓓ solve

6. Mr. Evans called the police when he saw the _____ break into a store.
   - Ⓐ emperor
   - Ⓑ palm
   - Ⓒ perspiration
   - Ⓓ burglar

7. My brother is a _____ runner and wins most of his races.
   - Ⓐ swift
   - Ⓑ grumpy
   - Ⓒ massive
   - Ⓓ cautious

8. Wes likes to use his _____ to make up stories.
   - Ⓐ business
   - Ⓑ homework
   - Ⓒ orbits
   - Ⓓ imagination

9. The most _____ part of the circus was the tight-rope walker.
   - Ⓐ exciting
   - Ⓑ dull
   - Ⓒ timid
   - Ⓓ make-believe

10. Father ran out the door in _____ because he was late for work.
    - Ⓐ frisky
    - Ⓑ haste
    - Ⓒ thunder
    - Ⓓ persuing

Overall Assessment 1, Page 2

Darken the letter of the word that means the same, or about the same, as the boldfaced word.

11. a **timid** child
- Ⓐ very happy
- Ⓑ too noisy
- Ⓒ easily frightened
- Ⓓ helpful

12. pursuing the dog
- Ⓐ feeding
- Ⓑ washing
- Ⓒ chasing
- Ⓓ walking

13. a **sore** foot
- Ⓐ painful
- Ⓑ right
- Ⓒ healthy
- Ⓓ growing

14. heard a **thud**
- Ⓐ chirp
- Ⓑ ring
- Ⓒ thump
- Ⓓ song

Darken the letter of the correct answer.

15. Choose the homophone that correctly completes the sentence.
Jake went _____ the park.
- Ⓐ two
- Ⓑ too
- Ⓒ to
- Ⓓ toe

16. Which prefix can be added to the beginning of the word *lucky* to make a new word?
- Ⓐ un
- Ⓑ im
- Ⓒ dis
- Ⓓ re

17. Which suffix can be added to the end of the word *sing* to make a new word?
- Ⓐ er
- Ⓑ ly
- Ⓒ ful
- Ⓓ less

18. Which word would be between the guide words *cap* and *check*?
- Ⓐ canoe
- Ⓑ clue
- Ⓒ cheerful
- Ⓓ cautious

Overall Assessment 2

Darken the letter of the word that fits best in the sentence.

1. The Earth _____ around the Sun.
- Ⓐ rises
- Ⓑ orbits
- Ⓒ depths
- Ⓓ dove

2. Lava is _____ rock that rises up and flows out of a volcano.
- Ⓐ cheerful
- Ⓑ ecosystem
- Ⓒ molten
- Ⓓ discovered

3. The _____ of sandpaper feels rough.
- Ⓐ surface
- Ⓑ electricity
- Ⓒ wound
- Ⓓ nutrients

4. Chou saw _____ flash from a stormy cloud.
- Ⓐ thunder
- Ⓑ lightning
- Ⓒ rain
- Ⓓ sleet

5. Nakita used a _____ to read under her bed covers after her mother turned off the light.
- Ⓐ business
- Ⓑ leash
- Ⓒ scratch
- Ⓓ flashlight

6. The _____ cat climbed a tree to get away from the barking dog.
- Ⓐ delicious
- Ⓑ sneaking
- Ⓒ frightened
- Ⓓ disguised

7. The water in the _____ stream came up to Anna's ankles.
- Ⓐ shallow
- Ⓑ equal
- Ⓒ massive
- Ⓓ seacoast

8. Our teacher said that she would _____ reading the book tomorrow.
- Ⓐ brave
- Ⓑ cautious
- Ⓒ cleanse
- Ⓓ continue

9. The girls were so hungry that they _____ two pizzas.
- Ⓐ consumed
- Ⓑ embraced
- Ⓒ scratch
- Ⓓ bent

10. Each forest is a complete _____ filled with plants and animals that live together.
- Ⓐ poncho
- Ⓑ ecosystem
- Ⓒ fuel
- Ⓓ cycles

Overall Assessment 2, Page 2

Darken the letter of the word that means the same, or about the same, as the boldfaced word.

11. a **frigid** wind
Ⓐ hot
Ⓑ light
Ⓒ cold
Ⓓ heavy

12. tramp in the woods
Ⓐ walk
Ⓑ lost
Ⓒ camp
Ⓓ shout

13. astonished by the news
Ⓐ bored
Ⓑ angry
Ⓒ fooled
Ⓓ surprised

14. take a **canoe** trip
Ⓐ camping
Ⓑ boat
Ⓒ hiking
Ⓓ vacation

Darken the letter of the correct answer.

15. Which prefix can be added to the beginning of the word *moved* to make a new word?
Ⓐ mis
Ⓑ dis
Ⓒ im
Ⓓ re

16. Which suffix can be added to the end of the word *quick* to make a new word?
Ⓐ ly
Ⓑ less
Ⓒ ful
Ⓓ able

17. Choose the homophone that correctly completes the sentence.
Gina and Rose said they would meet the team _____ for lunch.
Ⓐ their
Ⓑ there
Ⓒ they're
Ⓓ threw

18. Which word is the regular spelling for (kum´ pəs)?
Ⓐ campus
Ⓑ compose
Ⓒ compass
Ⓓ complete

Unit 1 Assessment

Darken the letter of the word that fits best in the sentence.

1. Heroes are ____ people who do something to help others.
   - Ⓐ silent
   - Ⓑ older
   - Ⓒ brave
   - Ⓓ noisy

2. The fastest swimmer will quickly take the ____ in a race.
   - Ⓐ rear
   - Ⓑ lead
   - Ⓒ bottom
   - Ⓓ top

3. Mrs. Jackson told us about many different ____ of dogs so we could choose the right kind of pet for us.
   - Ⓐ breeds
   - Ⓑ pictures
   - Ⓒ names
   - Ⓓ homes

4. The ____ kitten hid behind the sofa because it was scared.
   - Ⓐ lazy
   - Ⓑ tired
   - Ⓒ timid
   - Ⓓ active

5. Jack couldn't walk because his ____ was hurt.
   - Ⓐ ankle
   - Ⓑ elbow
   - Ⓒ shoulder
   - Ⓓ wrist

6. The heavy book fell on the floor with a loud ____.
   - Ⓐ clang
   - Ⓑ chirp
   - Ⓒ echo
   - Ⓓ thud

7. Erin put an ____ number of cookies in the boxes so they would be the same.
   - Ⓐ opposite
   - Ⓑ added
   - Ⓒ equal
   - Ⓓ extra

8. Mei Ling likes to read in the park because it is quiet and ____.
   - Ⓐ peaceful
   - Ⓑ loud
   - Ⓒ rainy
   - Ⓓ crowded

9. ____ are animals that belong in the cat family.
   - Ⓐ Horses
   - Ⓑ Felines
   - Ⓒ Elephants
   - Ⓓ Hamsters

10. It was ____ that the lost puppy came home after ten days.
    - Ⓐ usual
    - Ⓑ expected
    - Ⓒ terrible
    - Ⓓ unbelievable

Unit 1 Assessment, Page 2

Darken the letter of the word that fits best in the sentence.

11. The dog was trying to catch the cat it was _____ across the street.
- Ⓐ helping
- Ⓑ pursuing
- Ⓒ creeping
- Ⓓ digging

12. The _____ puppy tossed the ball into the air many times.
- Ⓐ lazy
- Ⓑ tired
- Ⓒ helpless
- Ⓓ frisky

13. "Your arm might feel _____ after you get this shot," said the doctor.
- Ⓐ loose
- Ⓑ sore
- Ⓒ firm
- Ⓓ relaxed

14. John found that the _____ box was too heavy for him to carry by himself.
- Ⓐ tiny
- Ⓑ messy
- Ⓒ massive
- Ⓓ silver

15. Mrs. Lee had to find a small dress for her _____ daughter.
- Ⓐ huge
- Ⓑ proud
- Ⓒ petite
- Ⓓ soft

16. Keeno has to walk his dog on a _____ or it will run away.
- Ⓐ leash
- Ⓑ bowl
- Ⓒ skate
- Ⓓ sidewalk

17. Sam could not reach the insect bite on his back to _____ it.
- Ⓐ pinch
- Ⓑ tickle
- Ⓒ water
- Ⓓ scratch

18. Dana _____ the knob on the toy too tightly and caused it to break.
- Ⓐ wound
- Ⓑ stirred
- Ⓒ raced
- Ⓓ kicked

19. The children were _____ because there was nothing to do.
- Ⓐ active
- Ⓑ laughing
- Ⓒ bored
- Ⓓ excited

20. "Would you _____ going to a movie today?" asked Mother.
- Ⓐ dislike
- Ⓑ enjoy
- Ⓒ trade
- Ⓓ learn

Natalie's Snake

Read the story. Think about the meanings of the words in bold type.

Natalie is my best friend. I am never **bored** when I visit her house. There is always something fun and exciting happening there. You see, Natalie has a pet snake! She calls her snake Rupert. Rupert is a **dull** brown color. In his forest home, he would look like the dried leaves on the ground. Rupert is very **timid** and hides in his glass house. Sometimes, Natalie will pick up Rupert and let the snake crawl up her arm.

She is not scared at all. I think Natalie is very **brave**. I am much more **cautious** because I do not like snakes. I will pet Rupert with just one finger.

Look back at the words in bold type. Use clues in the story to figure out the meaning of each word. Write each word on the line next to its meaning.

_____ **1.** easily frightened

_____ **2.** a feeling of not being interested

_____ **3.** using care

_____ **4.** not bright

_____ **5.** facing danger without fear

Name _____ Date _____

Antonyms

Antonyms are words with opposite meanings.
EXAMPLES: big—small   long—short   hard—easy

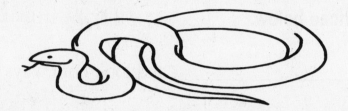

Match the words in the box with their antonyms listed below. Write the words on the lines.

| dull   brave   cautious   timid   bored |

_____ **1.** scared

_____ **2.** bold

_____ **3.** interested

_____ **4.** bright

_____ **5.** careless

Dictionary Skills

 The words in a dictionary are listed in **alphabetical order**.
EXAMPLE: break, color, cut, decide

Write the words in the box above in alphabetical order, one word on each line.

1. _____   **4.** _____

2. _____   **5.** _____

3. _____

Word Wise

dull	brave	cautious	timid	bored

Choose the word from the box that makes sense in the sentences below.

1. It is good to be _____ and look both ways before crossing a street.

2. Because Jason was _____, he was scared to talk in front of people.

3. The _____ police officer jumped into the water to save the child.

4. Mary was feeling _____ when her friends were away at summer camps.

5. Mr. Clark painted his garden fence a _____ green color.

Writing

Write your own story about a time you were brave. Use as many of the vocabulary words from the box as you can.

_____

_____

_____

_____

_____

Dog-Gone Friendly

Read the story. Think about the meanings of the words in bold type.

June and two of her friends took their dogs for a walk. The walk was not as fun as the friends thought it would be. June's dog, Captain, was the biggest dog. He wanted to be in the **lead**, so he raced ahead of everyone. June held the **leash** tightly, running to keep up with the huge dog. Abby's dog, Pepper, was the smallest. Pepper did not like to be left behind. Pepper would **tear** after Captain, running as fast as he could. Jack's dog, Angel, was very slow. Angel stopped often to sit down and **scratch** her ear. Before the walk was over, the dog's leashes got **wound** together. After much laughter, June and her friends were able to free the dogs.

Look back at the words in bold type. Use clues in the story to figure out the meaning of each word. Write each word on the line next to its meaning.

_____ **1.** to move quickly

_____ **2.** to rub to stop an itch

_____ **3.** wrapped around

_____ **4.** the first place

_____ **5.** a strap for holding an animal

Multiple Meanings

Some words have more than one meaning. You can use clues in the sentence to tell which meaning the word has.

EXAMPLE: leaves

meaning A: goes away. John **leaves** for camp next week.

meaning B: more than one leaf. Mom spent the morning raking **leaves**.

Write the letter of the correct meaning next to each sentence.

wound

meaning A: wrapped around

meaning B: a cut to the body

_____ **1.** The doctor looked at Ken's wound.

_____ **2.** Tran wound up the hose before cutting the grass.

lead

meaning A: the first place

meaning B: a kind of metal

_____ **3.** A long time ago, dishes were made out of lead.

_____ **4.** The fastest horse took the lead in the race.

tear

meaning A: to move quickly

meaning B: a drop of liquid from the eye

_____ **5.** My dog will tear out of the house when I come home from school.

_____ **6.** Lana wiped a tear from her eye.

Word Wise

lead	tear	wound	leash	scratch

Rewrite each sentence. Use one of the words from the box in place of a word or phrase in the sentence.

1. Mother does not like it when we move quickly around the house.

_____

2. The old dog began to rub an itch on its ear.

_____

3. When the children lined up, Myra was in the front.

_____

4. Fred wrapped a rope swing around the tree branch.

_____

5. John always walks his dog on a strap.

_____

Writing

Write your own story about a time you walked a dog or saw a dog being walked. Use as many of the vocabulary words from the box as you can.

_____

_____

_____

_____

_____

Name _____   Date _____

All About Dogs

Read the story. Think about the meanings of the words in bold type.

There are hundreds of **breeds** of dogs. These different kinds of dogs are divided into groups such as sporting dogs, hounds, and toy dogs. A dog can be **petite** like the Chihuahua, which is about the size of a pigeon.

Another dog can be large like the Irish Wolfhound, which may stand nearly three feet high. One of the most **massive** dogs is the Saint Bernard. These heavy dogs can weigh more than 200 pounds! Each year of a dog's life is **equal** to about seven years of a person's life. That means a ten-year-old dog is the same age as a seventy-year-old person. But no matter the age, people who own dogs **enjoy** having a pet that they can love.

Look back at the words in bold type. Use clues in the story to figure out the meaning of each word. Write each word on the line next to its meaning.

_____   **1.** being the same

_____   **2.** special kinds of plants or animals

_____   **3.** very big

_____   **4.** very small

_____   **5.** to get joy from

Synonyms

A **synonym** is a word that has the same, or almost the same, meaning as another word.

EXAMPLES: small—little   happy—glad   begin—start

Write the letter of the synonym beseide each word.

_____ **1.** petite   A. like

_____ **2.** equal   B. kinds

_____ **3.** enjoy   C. same

_____ **4.** breeds   D. large

_____ **5.** massive   E. small

Dictionary Skills

Guide words are at the top of each page in a dictionary. Guide words tell the first and last entry words listed on the page. Every word listed on the page comes between the guide words.

EXAMPLE:

Guide words: **whip**   **wish**

Entry words on page: white, who, wind

Darken the circle for the correct answer.

1. Which word would be between the guide words *egg* and *enter*?

Ⓐ equal   Ⓑ each   Ⓒ enjoy   Ⓓ edge

2. Which word would be between the guide words *march* and *meet*?

Ⓐ menu   Ⓑ massive   Ⓒ mend   Ⓓ maple

3. Which word would be between the guide words *breath* and *bride*?

Ⓐ breeds   Ⓑ branch   Ⓒ broke   Ⓓ brake

Word Wise

| breeds | petite | enjoy | equal | massive |

Choose the word from the box that makes sense in the sentences below.

1. There were many _____ of dogs at the dog show.

2. One kind of dog is so _____ that it can fit in one hand.

3. The _____ desk took up most of the room.

4. To make the teams _____, the teacher put seven people in each group.

5. Mary will _____ reading this book because it is by her favorite writer.

Writing

Write your own story about your favorite kind of dog. Use as many of the vocabulary words from the box as you can.

_____

_____

_____

_____

_____

_____

_____

_____

_____

The Trouble with Pets

Read the story. Think about the meanings of the words in bold type.

Jesse was on her way out the door when the cat raced past her. The dog dashed after the cat and knocked into Jesse. Jesse fell to the floor with a noisy **thud**.

"Ouch! My **ankle**!" she cried.

Jesse's dad came running when he heard the sound of Jessie falling. "What happened?" he asked.

"The dog is **pursuing** the cat. He bumped into me during the chase and knocked me over. I think I hurt my ankle when I fell," Jesse answered.

Mr. Andrews bent down and felt the place above Jesse's foot. "I'm sure you didn't **damage** your ankle. But it may be **sore** and hurt when you walk for a few days. Now, you better go find your pets before they get into more trouble."

Look back at the words in bold type. Use clues in the story to figure out the meaning of each word. Write each word on the line next to its meaning.

_____ **1.** harm

_____ **2.** painful; hurting

_____ **3.** the part of the body where the foot and leg meet

_____ **4.** a heavy sound

_____ **5.** following in order to catch

Word Groups

Words can be grouped by how they are alike.
EXAMPLE: types of dogs: poodle, Irish setter, beagle

Read each group of words. Think about how they are alike. Write the word from the box that best completes each group.

> ankle   pursuing   thud   damage   sore

1. harm, hurt, _____

2. elbow, knee, _____

3. hurting, painful, _____

4. thump, crash, _____

5. chasing, catching, _____

Dictionary Skills

A **syllable** is a part of a word that is pronounced at one time. Dictionary entry words are divided into syllables to show how they can be divided at the end of a writing line. A hyphen (-) is placed between syllables to separate them.
EXAMPLE: animal   an-i-mal

Find each word in a dictionary. Then, write each word with a hyphen between each syllable.

1. thud _____

2. pursuing _____

3. sore _____

4. damage _____

5. ankle _____

Word Wise

| sore | thud | ankle | damage | pursuing |

Choose the word from the box that makes sense in the sentences below.

1. The book made a _____ when it hit the floor.

2. Amy twisted her _____ when she slipped

and fell.

3. The children _____

each other were playing a game of tag.

4. The rain leaked through the roof and caused

_____ to the wall.

5. My elbow was _____ after I bumped it.

Writing

Write your own story about a time you got hurt. Use as many of the vocabulary words from the box as you can.

_____

_____

_____

_____

_____

_____

_____

Purr-fect Pets

Read the story. Think about the meanings of the words in bold type.

I think cats make the best pets. They take very little care. All they need is food, water, a sandbox, and love. Cats **cleanse** their fur by licking it. All **felines** also make a purring sound when they are happy. It is a very **peaceful** sound that makes me happy, too.

My cat is named Toby. When he was a kitten, Toby was very **frisky**. He had **unbelievable** amounts of energy. He could play and play. But now Toby is old. He spends most of his days sleeping on a chair.

Look back at the words in bold type. Use clues in the story to figure out the meaning of each word. Write each word on the line next to its meaning.

_____ **1.** cats

_____ **2.** not easily thought to be true

_____ **3.** calming

_____ **4.** active

_____ **5.** clean

Dictionary Skills

A dictionary can help you find out how to say, or pronounce, a word. A dictionary has a **pronunciation key** that lists the symbols for each sound. It also gives a familiar word in which the sound is heard. A pronunciation key usually appears on every other page of the dictionary.

a	add	i	it	o͝o	took	oi	oil
ā	ace	ī	ice	o͞o	pool	ou	pout
â	care	o	odd	u	up	ng	ring
ä	palm	ō	open	û	burn	th	thin
e	end	ô	order	yo͞o	fuse	t̶h̶	this
ē	equal					zh	vision

ə = { a in *above*   e in *sicken*   i in *possible*
      o in *melon*   u in *circus* }

EXAMPLE: kitten (kit´ ən)

Use the pronunciation key to help you say the vocabulary words in parentheses ( ) in the sentences below. Write the regular spelling for each word in ( ).

1. The newspaper had many ads for (fē´ līnz).

_____

2. The nurse had to (klenz) the cut on my finger to get the dirt out.

_____

3. The (fris´ kē) cat chased after the ball of yarn.

_____

4. It was (ən bə lē´ və bəl) to see how fast people ate during the

pie-eating contest. _____

5. The house is very (pēs´ fəl) after the children go to bed.

_____

Word Wise

cleanse	frisky	felines	peaceful	unbelievable

Rewrite each sentence. Use one of the words from the box in place of a word or phrase in the sentence. You may use more than one word in a sentence.

1. Gina's horse could do tricks that were not to be believed.

_____

2. The active puppy raced around the yard.

_____

3. Many cats like to be left alone.

_____

4. Sue found the park quiet and calm after a visit to the noisy city.

_____

5. The nurse had to clean the dirt from Rachel's eye.

_____

Writing

Write your own story about a cat you know or have seen. Use as many of the vocabulary words from the box as you can.

_____

_____

_____

_____

_____

Unit 2 Assessment

Darken the letter of the word that means the same, or about the same, as the boldfaced word.

1. **disguised** as a super hero
   - Ⓐ looked like
   - Ⓑ talked like
   - Ⓒ walked like
   - Ⓓ spoke like

2. **discovered** a secret
   - Ⓐ showed
   - Ⓑ heard
   - Ⓒ found out
   - Ⓓ told

3. **embraced** each other
   - Ⓐ waved to
   - Ⓑ hugged
   - Ⓒ shouted at
   - Ⓓ carried

4. **sneaking** up behind
   - Ⓐ moving quietly
   - Ⓑ moving loudly
   - Ⓒ moving quickly
   - Ⓓ moving wildly

5. **emperor** of the land
   - Ⓐ helper
   - Ⓑ owner
   - Ⓒ ruler
   - Ⓓ farmer

6. **received** a package
   - Ⓐ opened
   - Ⓑ got
   - Ⓒ found
   - Ⓓ mailed

7. a **rare** book
   - Ⓐ not often seen
   - Ⓑ well loved
   - Ⓒ unread
   - Ⓓ written

8. look for **clues**
   - Ⓐ pictures
   - Ⓑ hints
   - Ⓒ words
   - Ⓓ places

9. birthday **gift**
   - Ⓐ cake
   - Ⓑ party
   - Ⓒ card
   - Ⓓ present

10. left in **haste**
    - Ⓐ quickly
    - Ⓑ loudly
    - Ⓒ slowly
    - Ⓓ happily

Name _____ Date _____

Darken the letter of the word that means the same, or about the same, as the boldfaced word.

11. heard a **burglar**
Ⓐ laugh
Ⓑ noise
Ⓒ animal
Ⓓ robber

16. two **errors**
Ⓐ mistakes
Ⓑ ideas
Ⓒ drawings
Ⓓ jobs

12. solve a problem
Ⓐ answer
Ⓑ make
Ⓒ uncover
Ⓓ write

17. a **make-believe** story
Ⓐ easy
Ⓑ difficult
Ⓒ not good
Ⓓ not real

13. a **foolish** story
Ⓐ long
Ⓑ hard
Ⓒ silly
Ⓓ wonderful

18. various kinds of clothes
Ⓐ cotton
Ⓑ bright
Ⓒ several
Ⓓ dirty

14. a **swift** runner
Ⓐ tired
Ⓑ fast
Ⓒ slow
Ⓓ strange

19. exciting news
Ⓐ interesting
Ⓑ horrible
Ⓒ helpful
Ⓓ readable

15. an interesting **character**
Ⓐ place to visit
Ⓑ person in a book
Ⓒ story in a newspaper
Ⓓ costume in a play

20. a **business** card
Ⓐ birthday
Ⓑ get-well
Ⓒ job
Ⓓ playing

Grandma's Stories

Read the story. Think about the meanings of the words in bold type.

Lena's grandma told great stories. Lena and her sister especially liked the different ways their grandma told "Little Red Riding Hood." The **crafty** wolf was always looking for a way to trick Red! In one story, the wolf **disguised** himself as a bottled-water salesman. In another story, the wolf painted himself to look like a tree. "No! No! Don't trust him, Red!" Lena and her sister would yell when the wolf was **sneaking** close to Red. Then, they shivered and **embraced** each other in a big hug. But in all of Grandma's stories, Red always **discovered** the wolf's trick and sent him back into the forest.

Look back at the words in bold type. Use clues in the story to figure out the meaning of each word. Write each word on the line next to its meaning.

_____ **1.** skillful in tricking

_____ **2.** held in the arms

_____ **3.** found out

_____ **4.** moving in a secret way

_____ **5.** changed the way one looks

Base Words

Base words are words without any endings or other word parts added to them. Some endings are **ing**, **ed**, **s**, and **y**. Sometimes the spelling of the base word changes when an ending is added to it.

EXAMPLES:
open	opening
cry	cried
step	steps
trick	tricky

Write the base word of each word below. Then, use the base word in a sentence.

1. embraced _____

_____

2. crafty _____

_____

3. discovered _____

_____

4. sneaking _____

_____

5. disguised _____

_____

Word Wise

crafty	sneaking	disguised	embraced	discovered

Rewrite each sentence. Use one of the words from the box in place of a word or phrase in the sentence.

1. Tim was moving in a secret way close to the birds so he would not scare them away.

_____

2. Marie found out that her computer had a bug.

_____

3. That tricky fish just took my bait!

_____

4. Matt changed the way he looked so that he could spy on his sister.

_____

5. Mrs. Hugo hugged her son when he got home from school.

_____

Writing

Write your own story about a way the wolf in "Little Red Riding Hood" tries to trick Red. Use as many of the vocabulary words from the box as you can.

_____

_____

_____

_____

_____

The Emperor's Birthday

Read the story. Think about the meanings of the words in bold type.

Long ago, a kind **emperor** was giving a huge party for his birthday. Everyone in the empire was invited. The ruler even offered a prize to the person who brought him the best **gift**.

On the day of his party, the emperor **received** many gifts for his birthday. Some people gave the emperor fine **silk** cloth. Others gave him **rare** books and jewels that were hard to find. The emperor thanked each person, but he had not found the best gift. Finally, a small boy held out a little bird. The emperor looked down and asked, "And why do you give me a bird?"

The boy answered, "Even an emperor must get lonely at times. This bird will be your friend."

The emperor smiled. At long last, he had found the best gift—friendship! The emperor gave the boy all the other birthday gifts.

Look back at the words in bold type. Use clues in the story to figure out the meaning of each word. Write each word on the line next to its meaning.

_____ **1.** something given

_____ **2.** not often seen or found

_____ **3.** soft, shiny threads made by worms

_____ **4.** a ruler or leader

_____ **5.** got something

Analogies

An **analogy** shows how two words go together in the same way as two other words.
EXAMPLE: <u>Kitten</u> is to <u>cat</u> as <u>puppy</u> is to <u>dog</u>.

Think about how the words in the first pair go together. Write the word from the box to complete the analogy.

> silk   gift   rare   received   emperor

1. <u>Much</u> is to <u>little</u> as <u>common</u> is to _____.

2. <u>Kingdom</u> is to <u>king</u> as <u>empire</u> is to _____.

3. <u>Cup</u> is to <u>glass</u> as <u>present</u> is to _____.

4. <u>Rough</u> is to <u>sandpaper</u> as <u>smooth</u> is to _____.

5. <u>Stopped</u> is to <u>started</u> as <u>gave</u> is to _____.

Dictionary Skills

 The words in a dictionary are listed in **alphabetical order**.
EXAMPLE: bird, friend, party, prize

Write the vocabulary words from the box above in alphabetical order, one word on each line.

1. _____

2. _____

3. _____

4. _____

5. _____

Word Wise

silk	gift	rare	received	emperor

Choose the word from the box that makes sense in the sentences below.

1. Ray hunts for _____ marbles to add to his collection.

2. Mrs. Todd bought a beautiful _____ blouse.

3. A ruler in China was called an _____ many years ago.

4. Rita _____ a letter from her grandmother in the mail.

5. Carl could hardly wait to open the birthday _____ from his best friend.

Writing

Imagine that you are an emperor. Write your own story about a gift you would like to get. Use as many of the vocabulary words from the box as you can.

_____

_____

_____

_____

_____

_____

_____

Mia's Mystery

Read the story. Think about the meanings of the words in bold type.

Mia loves to read mystery books. She reads very slowly to look for **clues**. If Mia reads in **haste**, she is afraid that she might miss the hints to see who did the crime. Then, she will not be able to **solve** the mystery on her own.

One time when Mia was reading late at night, she thought she heard a **burglar** breaking into the house. When Mia crept downstairs, she found that her brother had gone to the kitchen to get a snack to eat. Mia felt **foolish** when she told her brother about her silly idea. He just laughed and said that Mia had read too many mysteries.

Look back at the words in bold type. Use clues in the story to figure out the meaning of each word. Write each word on the line next to its meaning.

_____ **1.** unwise; silly

_____ **2.** to find an answer to

_____ **3.** hints that help find an answer

_____ **4.** a person who breaks into a house

_____ **5.** quickness in moving or acting

Synonyms

A **synonym** is a word that has the same, or almost the same, meaning as another word.
EXAMPLES: story—tale   happy—glad

Choose the word from the box that matches its synonym. Write the word on the line.

clues   solve   haste   burglar   foolish

1. quickness _____

2. hints _____

3. silly _____

4. robber _____

5. answer _____

Dictionary Skills

The words in a dictionary are listed in **alphabetical order**.
EXAMPLE: read, school, spelling, success

Write the vocabulary words from the box above in alphabetical order, one word on each line.

1. _____

2. _____

3. _____

4. _____

5. _____

Name _____ Date _____

Word Wise

clues   haste   solve   burglar   foolish

Choose the word from the box that makes sense in the sentences below.

7

1. The footprints were _____ that helped John find out how his room got so messy.

2. The police caught the _____ with a bag full of stolen jewels.

3. It was _____ for Ryan to plan a party without asking his father first.

4. The children ran out the door in _____ so they would not be late for the bus.

5. Meisha was the first person in the class to _____ the math problem.

Writing

Write your own mystery. Use as many of the vocabulary words from the box as you can.

_____

_____

_____

_____

_____

_____

Rabbit Stories

Read the story. Think about the meanings of the words in bold type.

Many years ago, Native Americans believed that animals talked and acted like people. They told many **legends** about the lives of the animals. Rabbit was a favorite **character** in these stories. Rabbit was a **swift** runner because of his long legs. He often delivered messages to all the animals. Rabbit also played many tricks on other animals. However, the tricks **usually** did not work, and Rabbit would get into trouble. Rabbit never did learn from his **errors**. Somehow he would find a new way to get into trouble.

Look back at the words in bold type. Use clues in the story to figure out the meaning of each word. Write each word on the line next to its meaning.

_____ **1.** a person in a book, play, or story

_____ **2.** often; commonly

_____ **3.** able to move quickly

_____ **4.** mistakes

_____ **5.** stories passed down for many years

Word Groups

Words can be grouped by how they are alike.
EXAMPLE: types of animals: mammals, fish, birds

Read each group of words. Think about how they are alike. Write the word from the box that best completes each group.

| errors | swift | legends | usually | character |

1. plot, setting, _____
2. myths, fables, _____
3. mistakes, problems, _____
4. quick, fast, _____
5. commonly, often, _____

Dictionary Skills

Guide words are at the top of each page in a dictionary. Guide words tell the first and last entry words listed on the page. Every word listed on the page comes between the guide words.
EXAMPLE: **tall**   **treat**
tame, tea, teach, track

Darken the circle for the correct answer.

1. Which word would be between the guide words *cell* and *clap*?
   Ⓐ characters   Ⓑ clean   Ⓒ ceiling   Ⓓ coffee

2. Which word would be between the guide words *end* and *escape*?
   Ⓐ exit   Ⓑ eagle   Ⓒ errors   Ⓓ every

3. Which word would be between the guide words *left* and *less*?
   Ⓐ letter   Ⓑ least   Ⓒ lever   Ⓓ legends

Name _____   Date _____

Word Wise

| errors | swift | legends | usually | character |

Choose the word from the box that makes sense in the sentences below.

1. Sam _____ practices on his skateboard after school.

2. Who is your favorite _____ in the book *Super Fudge* by Judy Bloom?

3. The dog was such a _____ runner that it was hard to catch.

4. There are many _____ about the famous woodsman Paul Bunyan and his blue ox, Babe.

5. I made only two _____ on my math test.

Writing

Write your own story about a talking animal. Use as many of the vocabulary words from the box as you can.

_____
_____
_____
_____
_____
_____
_____
_____

www.svschoolsupply.com
© Steck-Vaughn Company

38

Unit 2, Lesson 9, Page 3
Vocabulary Skills 3, SV 6902-7

Write a Story!

Read the story. Think about the meanings of the words in bold type.

When you write a story, you need to use your **imagination**. Picture in your mind a character that would be interesting to read about. The character can be real or **make-believe**. Next, decide what your character is like. How does your character look? What does your character like to do? Maybe your character could have a special job or **business**. Then, think of **various** story problems. Choose the idea that you think would be the most **exciting**. Now, find a way for your character to solve the problem. It is important to have a good ending that clears up the problem.

Look back at the words in bold type. Use clues in the story to figure out the meaning of each word. Write each word on the line next to its meaning.

_____ **1.** the work that a person does

_____ **2.** not real

_____ **3.** many

_____ **4.** the thinking of pictures and ideas that are not real

_____ **5.** causing an interest

Dictionary Skills

A dictionary can help you find out how to say, or pronounce, a word. A dictionary has a **pronunciation key** that lists the symbols for each sound. It also gives a familiar word in which the sound is heard. A pronunciation key usually appears on every other page of the dictionary.

a	add	i	it	o͝o	took	oi	oil
ā	ace	ī	ice	o͞o	pool	ou	pout
â	care	o	odd	u	up	ng	ring
ä	palm	ō	open	û	burn	th	thin
e	end	ô	order	yo͞o	fuse	~~th~~	this
ē	equal					zh	vision

ə = { a in *above* e in *sicken* i in *possible*
      { o in *melon* u in *circus*

EXAMPLE: kitten (kit´ ən)

Use the pronunciation key to help you say the vocabulary words in parentheses ( ) in the sentences below. Write the regular spelling for each word in ( ).

1. The characters in fairy tales are (māk´ bi lēv´).

_____

2. Sue used her (i maj´ ə nā´ shən) to make up all kinds of friends.

_____

3. The most (ek sī´ ting) part of the day was when we went swimming.

_____

4. Todd has a (biz´ nis) that makes wooden trains.

_____

5. The map shows (vâr´ ē əs) ways to get to the store.

_____

Word Wise

| business | exciting | various | imagination | make-believe |

Choose the word from the box that
makes sense in the sentences below.

1. Rose went shopping to buy

   _____ things

   she needed to play soccer.

2. Sailing in a boat is very fun and _____ .

3. We dress up in costumes to become _____

   characters.

4. My father has been in the painting _____

   for many years.

5. The teacher asked us to use our _____

   to think about what it might be like to be a fish.

Writing

**Write your own story about a character who has a toy shop. Use as many
of the vocabulary words from the box as you can.**

_____

_____

_____

_____

_____

Unit 3 Assessment

Darken the letter of the word that fits best in the sentence.

1. When the school bell rang, the students left the _____.
   - Ⓐ bedroom
   - Ⓑ classroom
   - Ⓒ zoo
   - Ⓓ restaurant

2. Jeff could not do his math _____ because he left his book at school.
   - Ⓐ chores
   - Ⓑ jokes
   - Ⓒ pencils
   - Ⓓ homework

3. Ned likes to go to the _____ to watch the planes land and take off.
   - Ⓐ airport
   - Ⓑ store
   - Ⓒ school
   - Ⓓ library

4. Mr. Edwards hung some of the pictures outside his door in the _____ for everyone to see as they walked by.
   - Ⓐ hallway
   - Ⓑ closet
   - Ⓒ desk
   - Ⓓ cafeteria

5. The _____ air helped keep the snow on the ground for several days.
   - Ⓐ party
   - Ⓑ frigid
   - Ⓒ smoky
   - Ⓓ warm

6. It is important to _____ every day to keep the body strong and healthy.
   - Ⓐ read
   - Ⓑ dream
   - Ⓒ study
   - Ⓓ exercise

7. Oscar walked to the _____ to buy some bananas.
   - Ⓐ garage
   - Ⓑ restaurant
   - Ⓒ supermarket
   - Ⓓ ocean

8. "Just walking out in this heat makes the _____ roll down my face," said Peter.
   - Ⓐ perspiration
   - Ⓑ painting
   - Ⓒ shampoo
   - Ⓓ shivers

9. I would have forgotten my science book if Mom had not _____ me before I left the house.
   - Ⓐ whispered
   - Ⓑ reminded
   - Ⓒ coached
   - Ⓓ written

10. Laura was _____ when she won first prize in the poetry contest.
   - Ⓐ tasty
   - Ⓑ angry
   - Ⓒ hopeful
   - Ⓓ astonished

Unit 3 Assessment, Page 2

Darken the letter of the word that fits best in the sentence.

11. When Rick was at camp, he wanted to go home because he was _____.
   Ⓐ silent
   Ⓑ lazy
   Ⓒ homesick
   Ⓓ tough

12. Grandpa's favorite _____ memory was when he caught a fish that was bigger than the one his dad caught.
   Ⓐ childhood
   Ⓑ circus
   Ⓒ business
   Ⓓ building

13. Sonya held out a diamond in the _____ of her hand.
   Ⓐ finger
   Ⓑ purse
   Ⓒ ring
   Ⓓ palm

14. Mrs. Paterson _____ over to pick up some paper that had fallen on the floor.
   Ⓐ bent
   Ⓑ twisted
   Ⓒ hopped
   Ⓓ swam

15. A white _____ is a sign that means "peace."
   Ⓐ flower
   Ⓑ moon
   Ⓒ dove
   Ⓓ shirt

16. Beth was _____ to stay inside because it was too hot in the sun.
   Ⓐ serious
   Ⓑ lonely
   Ⓒ unhappy
   Ⓓ content

17. Zeke signed up to take a _____ trip down a river.
   Ⓐ horse
   Ⓑ canoe
   Ⓒ singing
   Ⓓ hiking

18. Rita could tell that Jay was _____ because he was frowning.
   Ⓐ grumpy
   Ⓑ excited
   Ⓒ eager
   Ⓓ funny

19. The _____ helped Maria find her way when she got lost.
   Ⓐ backpack
   Ⓑ pole
   Ⓒ compass
   Ⓓ rails

20. As soon as it began to rain, Steve put on his _____.
   Ⓐ sweater
   Ⓑ mitt
   Ⓒ smile
   Ⓓ poncho

No Time for Baseball

Read the story. Think about the meanings of the words in bold type.

I waved good-bye to my teacher and raced out of the **classroom**. My friends were waiting for me outside the door.

"We're going to the playground to play **baseball**," Chou said. "Do you want to go with us?

"Not today," I answered. "I have to go to the library and do my **homework**."

"Homework! Why do you want to do it now?" asked Tina.

"My mom helps airplanes land at the **airport**. She said that I could go watch her work if I get all my work done. So I need to get it done as quickly as I can." I gave another wave and walked quickly down the **hallway**.

Look back at the words in bold type. Use clues in the story to figure out the meaning of each word. Write each word on the line next to its meaning.

_____ **1.** a game played with a bat and ball

_____ **2.** a place where airplanes take off and land

_____ **3.** work given at school to be done at home

_____ **4.** a part of a building used to go between rooms

_____ **5.** a room in which classes are held

Compound Words

A **compound word** is a word formed by putting two or more words together.

EXAMPLES: playground, birthday

Draw a line to match one word from Column A with one from Column B to make a compound word. Use each word only once. Write each new word in a box. Then, draw a picture to show its meaning.

Column A	Column B
air	work
class	way
hall	port
base	room
home	ball

1.

2.

3.

4.

5.

Word Wise

airport   hallway   baseball   classroom   homework

Rewrite each sentence. Use one of the words from the box in place of a word or phrase in the sentence. Make any changes needed.

1. The teacher turned on the lights in the room where classes are held.

_____

2. Mr. Ruiz gave us ten math problems to work at home.

_____

3. We drove to the place where planes land to pick up my grandmother.

_____

4. Larry and his friends went to the park to play a game with a ball and a bat.

_____

5. The children walked quietly in the place between the rooms in a building.

_____

Writing

Write your own story about something fun you did after school one day. Use as many of the vocabulary words from this lesson as you can.

_____

_____

_____

_____

_____

Too Hot!

Read the story. Think about the meanings of the words in bold type.

The day was really hot—100 degrees in the shade! I had wet drops of **perspiration** on my forehead. I love cool weather, but I dislike the heat. Jill wanted to do a rain dance, but it was too hot for **exercise**. A workout like that is for chilly weather. Andy wanted to walk to the beach. But I couldn't stand to **tramp** in the heat. I think my idea was the best. I wanted to spend the day at the **supermarket**. Why go to a food store, you ask? The coolers! Their **frigid** air would cool us off in no time flat!

Look back at the words in bold type. Use clues in the story to figure out the meaning of each word. Write each word on the line next to its meaning.

_____ **1.** working out to make the body better

_____ **2.** very cold

_____ **3.** a large store where food is sold

_____ **4.** to travel by foot

_____ **5.** sweat

Name _____ Date _____

Synonyms

Synonyms are words that have the same, or almost the same, meaning.
EXAMPLES: story—tale   happy—glad

Choose the word from the box that matches its synonym. Write the word on the line.

> frigid   tramp   exercise   perspiration   supermarket

1. work out _____

2. cold _____

3. food store _____

4. sweat _____

5. walk _____

Dictionary Skills

A **syllable** is a part of a word that is pronounced at one time. Dictionary entry words are divided into syllables to show how they can be divided at the end of a writing line. A hyphen (-) is placed between syllables to separate them.
EXAMPLE: animal   an-i-mal

Find each word in a dictionary. Then, write each word with a hyphen between each syllable.

1. exercise _____

2. tramp _____

3. frigid _____

4. perspiration _____

5. supermarket _____

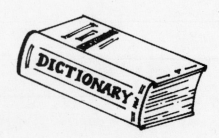

Word Wise

| tramp | frigid | exercise | perspiration | supermarket |

Choose the word from the box that makes sense in the sentences below.

1. The hot sun caused the _____ to roll down

Terry's face.

2. Hua did not want to go outside to play because of

the snow and _____ wind.

3. We had to _____ through

the woods to find the wild berries.

4. Mother went to the _____ to buy some food

for dinner.

5. We always start soccer practice with _____

to warm up our bodies.

Writing

Write your own story about an interesting way to stay cool in hot weather. Use as many of the vocabulary words from the box as you can.

_____

_____

_____

_____

_____

My Aunt Judith

Read the story. Think about the meanings of the words in bold type.

I was looking through a magazine when I saw a beautiful picture of a **seacoast**. The ocean scene **reminded** me of a time in my **childhood** when I was seven years old. My parents and I went to visit Aunt Judith, who lived near the ocean. Aunt Judith was a kind woman who liked to paint. She let me use some of her paints to make my own picture. Aunt Judith was **astonished** at how well I painted. I ended up staying a whole week alone with my aunt. I was **homesick** at first, but Aunt Judith was so much fun that I soon forgot about how much I missed home.

Look back at the words in bold type. Use clues in the story to figure out the meaning of each word. Write each word on the line next to its meaning.

_____ **1.** very surprised

_____ **2.** the time in life when a person is a child

_____ **3.** feeling sad because of being away from home

_____ **4.** land that is near the sea

_____ **5.** made to think of something

A Crossword Puzzle

Use the clues and the words in the box to complete the crossword puzzle.

homesick   seacoast   astonished   reminded   childhood

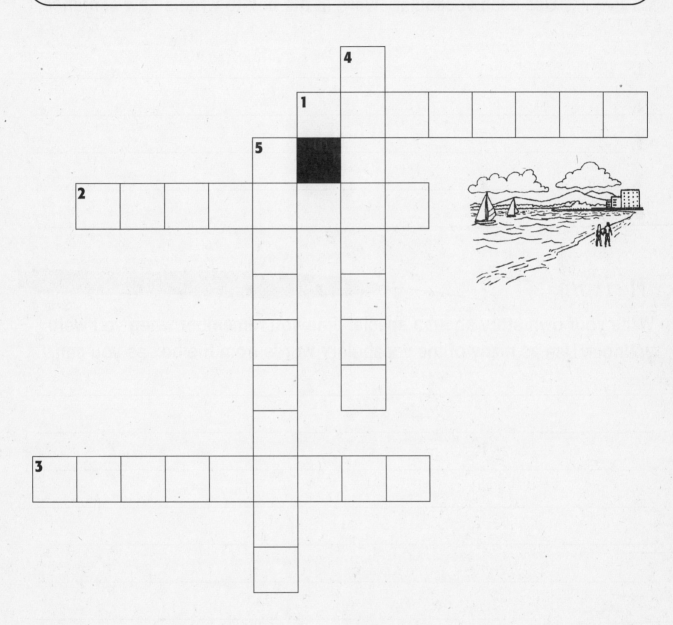

Across
1. helped to remember something
2. unhappy because of missing home
3. time when a person is very young

Down
4. land next to the ocean
5. surprised

Word Wise

homesick	seacoast	astonished	reminded	childhood

Use each vocabulary word in the box to write a new sentence.

1. _____

2. _____

3. _____

4. _____

5. _____

Writing

Write your own story about a special time you remember when you were younger. Use as many of the vocabulary words from the box as you can.

_____

_____

_____

_____

_____

_____

_____

_____

_____

The Dove

Read the story. Think about the meanings of the words in bold type.

I was walking around the lake when I stopped to rest by a tree. All of a sudden, I heard a cooing beside my foot. I was **amazed** to find a baby bird in the tall grass. I **bent** over and carefully picked it up with my hand. When I opened my hand, it sat quietly in my **palm**. Its gray color led me to think it was a **dove**. Soon, I heard more cooing. Other babies were in a nest above my head. The dove I was holding must have fallen out. I decided to put the baby back in its nest. I stood up and stepped onto a low tree branch. Carefully, I put the baby back in its nest. The dove must have been **content** and happy to be back home because I did not hear any more sounds.

Look back at the words in bold type. Use clues in the story to figure out the meaning of each word. Write each word on the line next to its meaning.

_____ **1.** happy and satisfied

_____ **2.** a kind of bird

_____ **3.** surprised

_____ **4.** moved the top part of the body forward and down

_____ **5.** the inside flat part of the hand

Multiple Meanings

Some words have more than one meaning. You can use clues in the sentence to tell which meaning the word has.

EXAMPLE: fish

meaning A: a group of animals that live in water. We eat fresh **fish** at the beach.

meaning B: to pull out. I had to **fish** some coins out of my purse.

Write the letter of the correct meaning next to each sentence.

content

meaning A: happy and satisfied
meaning B: all things inside

_____ **1.** The children were content to play a game on a rainy day.

_____ **2.** Everybody wanted to know the content of the locked box.

palm

meaning A: the inside flat part of the hand
meaning B: a kind of tree

_____ **3.** Some palm trees grow coconuts.

_____ **4.** The melted candy bar covered the palm of Domingo's hand.

dove

meaning A: a kind of bird
meaning B: did dive

_____ **5.** Jana held her breath and dove into the pool.

_____ **6.** The dove ate seeds from the bird feeder.

Word Wise

dove	bent	palm	amazed	content

Choose the word from the box that makes sense in the sentences below.

1. Clara _____ over to

pick a flower from her garden.

2. We were _____ by how many times the man

flipped when he was in the air.

3. Leon was so tired that he was _____ to read a

book the rest of the afternoon.

4. The _____ flew into a tree when Greg walked by.

5. The Chihuahua puppy was so small that Fran could hold it in the

_____ of her hand.

Writing

Write your own story about something that happened during a walk. Use as many of the vocabulary words from the box as you can.

_____

_____

_____

_____

_____

A Trip Down the River

Read the story. Think about the meanings of the words in bold type.

Dad and Grandpa are **outdoorsmen** who love to hike and camp. Once a year, they plan a trip and take me with them. This year, we took a **canoe** trip down the Blue River. I got to help paddle. We used a **compass** to make sure we were going the right way. Each night, we stopped to camp. Sleeping in the tent was so much fun. It was the best trip ever! Even when it rained, I did not get **grumpy**. I just put on a **poncho** and kept going.

Look back at the words in bold type. Use clues in the story to figure out the meaning of each word. Write each word on the line next to its meaning.

_____ **1.** in a bad mood

_____ **2.** people who like being in nature

_____ **3.** a kind of boat

_____ **4.** a coat that pulls over the head and keeps water away

_____ **5.** a tool that tells direction

Dictionary Skills

A dictionary can help you find out how to say, or pronounce, a word. A dictionary has a **pronunciation key** that lists the symbols for each sound. It also gives a familiar word in which the sound is heard. A pronunciation key usually appears on every other page of the dictionary.

a	add	i	it	o͝o	took	oi	oil
ā	ace	ī	ice	o͞o	pool	ou	pout
â	care	o	odd	u	up	ng	ring
ä	palm	ō	open	û	burn	th	thin
e	end	ô	order	yo͞o	fuse	t̶h̶	this
ē	equal					zh	vision

ə = { a in *above*   e in *sicken*   i in *possible*
      o in *melon*   u in *circus* }

EXAMPLE: kitten (kit´ ən)

Use the pronunciation key to help you say the vocabulary words in parentheses ( ) in the sentences below. Write the regular spelling for each word in ( ).

1. When Dan got lost in the woods, he used a (kum´ pəs) to find which

way to go. _____

2. Tina used a (kə no͞o´) to cross the lake.

_____

3. Cleaning her room always made Kim feel (grum´ pē).

_____

4. We like to think of ourselves as (out´ dôrz men´) because we go

camping several times each year. _____

5. Sandy put on a (pon´ chō) when it began to rain.

_____

Word Wise

canoe	grumpy	poncho	compass	outdoorsmen

Rewrite each sentence. Use one of the words from the box in place of a word or phrase in the sentence. Make any changes needed.

1. Anna and her dad were people who loved nature and spent time hiking through the woods each weekend.

   _____

2. The ship's captain used a tool to tell direction when the storm blew them off course.

   _____

3. Soon Lei tried to cheer up Jake when she saw that he was in a bad mood.

   _____

4. Many people who go to baseball games take a coat to keep off rain.

   _____

5. Grandpa said that he would take me for a ride in the little boat after lunch.

   _____

Writing

Write your own story about what you would like to do on a camping trip. Use as many of the vocabulary words from the box as you can.

   _____

   _____

   _____

   _____

Unit 4 Assessment

Darken the letter of the word that means the same, or about the same, as the boldfaced word.

1. **depths** of the ocean
   - Ⓐ highest part
   - Ⓑ widest part
   - Ⓒ shortest part
   - Ⓓ deepest part

2. a hard **surface**
   - Ⓐ outside
   - Ⓑ inside
   - Ⓒ bottom
   - Ⓓ middle

3. **molten** rock
   - Ⓐ small
   - Ⓑ frozen
   - Ⓒ melted
   - Ⓓ chipped

4. **orbits** the Sun
   - Ⓐ moves around
   - Ⓑ flies near
   - Ⓒ goes into
   - Ⓓ shines with

5. feeling **frightened**
   - Ⓐ hurt
   - Ⓑ scared
   - Ⓒ full
   - Ⓓ wonderful

6. turn off the **electricity**
   - Ⓐ road
   - Ⓑ noise
   - Ⓒ car
   - Ⓓ power

7. a **shallow** pond
   - Ⓐ dirty
   - Ⓑ clear
   - Ⓒ not deep
   - Ⓓ far away

8. beginning to **panic**
   - Ⓐ feel hurried
   - Ⓑ start laughing
   - Ⓒ be fearful
   - Ⓓ have fun

9. **continue** on the road
   - Ⓐ keep going
   - Ⓑ stop
   - Ⓒ ride
   - Ⓓ walk

10. a **cheerful** greeting
    - Ⓐ short
    - Ⓑ happy
    - Ⓒ steady
    - Ⓓ quick

Unit 4 Assessment, Page 2

Darken the letter of the word that means the same, or about the same, as the boldfaced word.

11. a **crooked** tree
- Ⓐ tall
- Ⓑ short
- Ⓒ straight
- Ⓓ bent

12. a **delicious** pie
- Ⓐ hot
- Ⓑ fruity
- Ⓒ tasty
- Ⓓ cooked

13. tart apples
- Ⓐ sour
- Ⓑ sweet
- Ⓒ rotten
- Ⓓ red

14. many different **varieties**
- Ⓐ flavors
- Ⓑ sizes
- Ⓒ weights
- Ⓓ kinds

15. consumed the muffins
- Ⓐ ate
- Ⓑ baked
- Ⓒ sold
- Ⓓ bought

16. familiar sights
- Ⓐ interesting
- Ⓑ different
- Ⓒ colorful
- Ⓓ well-known

17. the fire **smoldered**
- Ⓐ died
- Ⓑ smoked
- Ⓒ moved
- Ⓓ started

18. nutrients for the body
- Ⓐ food
- Ⓑ fat
- Ⓒ exercise
- Ⓓ harmful

19. cycles of the seasons
- Ⓐ weather
- Ⓑ kinds of clothing
- Ⓒ leaf changes
- Ⓓ repeated events

20. fuel for cooking
- Ⓐ something that smokes
- Ⓑ something that burns
- Ⓒ something that boils
- Ⓓ something that is eaten

The Earth

Read the story. Think about the meanings of the words in bold type.

What do you think it would be like to visit the stars and planets of the **universe**? Maybe you would like to visit our solar system first. As you know, the Earth **orbits** the Sun.

Then after you explored space, what do you think it would be like to visit the **depths** of the Earth? The hard **surface** of the Earth is very different from its center. If you could dig far down inside the Earth, you would find **molten** rock. It is so hot that rocks melt and move like water.

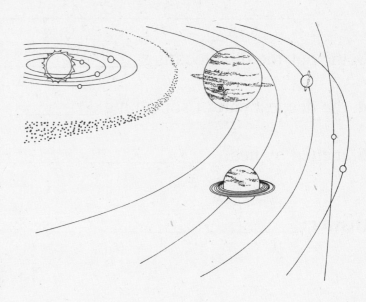

Look back at the words in bold type. Use clues in the story to figure out the meaning of each word. Write each word on the line next to its meaning.

_____ **1.** everything that is part of space, including stars and planets

_____ **2.** the outside of something

_____ **3.** melted by heat

_____ **4.** moves around something else

_____ **5.** the deepest part of something

Word Puzzle

Write a vocabulary word next to each definition. Then, use the numbered letters to answer the question, "What is the Sun?"

1. it moves in a circle around something else

___ ___ ___ ___ ___ ___
         1   2

2. everything that is part of space, including stars and planets

___ ___ ___ ___ ___ ___ ___ ___
      3   4

3. the outside of something ___ ___ ___ ___ ___ ___ ___
                                8   5

4. the deepest part of something ___ ___ ___ ___ ___ ___
                                      6

5. melted by heat ___ ___ ___ ___ ___
                 7

Answer: ___ ___ ___ ___ ___ ___ ___ ___ ___ .
      1   2   3   4   5   6   7   5   8

Word Wise

orbits   molten   depths   surface   universe

Choose the word from the box that makes sense in the sentences below.

1. The Earth _____ the Sun.

2. No one has visited the _____ of the ocean because it is so deep.

3. The _____ is made up of all the stars, planets, and everything else in space.

4. The _____ of the table was very dirty.

5. The lava that pours out of a volcano is _____ rock.

Writing

What do you think it would be like to travel in space? Write a story about what you would do and see. Use as many of the vocabulary words from the box as you can.

_____

_____

_____

_____

_____

_____

_____

The Storm

Read the story. Think about the meanings of the words in bold type.

Keesha looked out the window and saw big black clouds race toward her in the sky. Soon **lightning** flashed. Keesha began to count very slowly—1, 2, 3. Then, she heard the loud crash of **thunder**. The storm was about three miles away. Keesha was a little **frightened** because she did not like these kind of storms. She hoped her mother would be home soon. But Keesha knew what to do in case the **electricity** went off and she could not use the lights. Keesha began to look for the **flashlight**.

Look back at the words in bold type. Use clues in the story to figure out the meaning of each word. Write each word on the line next to its meaning.

_____ **1.** a form of energy made by people

_____ **2.** a flash of light in the sky

_____ **3.** a small light that uses batteries

_____ **4.** scared

_____ **5.** a loud sound that follows lightning

Make a Picture

How do you picture words? Sometimes the picture you draw in your mind can help you remember the meanings of words.
EXAMPLE: umbrella

Draw a picture for each of the vocabulary words below.

umbrella 	**3.** frightened
1. thunder	**4.** flashlight
2. lightning	**5.** electricity

Word Wise

thunder   lightning   frightened   electricity   flashlight

Rewrite each sentence. Use one of the words from the box in place of a word or phrase in the sentence.

1. Glen saw streaks of light flash across the sky.

_____

2. Then, he heard the loud crashing sound that followed.

_____

3. Glen wondered if the energy would go off so there would be no lights.

_____

4. He went to look for a small light with batteries.

_____

5. The light would keep him from feeling scared.

_____

Writing

Write your own story about a thunderstorm. Use as many of the vocabulary words from the box as you can.

_____

_____

_____

_____

_____

The Hike

Read the story. Think about the meanings of the words in bold type.

Joey and Ben went for a hike in the forest. They stepped on rocks to cross a **shallow** stream. Then, they took a left turn to climb a hill. The path was very **crooked** and not well marked. Before long, the two boys were lost in the twists and turns of the forest trail.

Joey and Ben did not know what to do. Joey thought they should **continue** on the same path. But Ben wanted to go back the way they had come. The boys ended up staying where they were and yelling loudly every five minutes. To Ben, it seemed as if they had been yelling for several hours, and he was beginning to **panic**. Joey remained **cheerful**. He believed that someone would find them. Suddenly, the boys heard a noise coming from the bushes. It was a forest ranger! Joey and Ben could now go home.

Look back at the words in bold type. Use clues in the story to figure out the meaning of each word. Write each word on the line next to its meaning.

_____ **1.** a feeling of fear that makes a person want to run away

_____ **2.** feeling happy

_____ **3.** to go on without stopping

_____ **4.** not straight

_____ **5.** not deep

Antonyms

Antonyms are words that have opposite meanings.
EXAMPLES: happy—sad   quickly—slowly   small—large

Match the words in the box with their antonyms. Write the words on the lines.

| panic   shallow   crooked   cheerful   continue |

1. straight _____

2. calm _____

3. sad _____

4. stop _____

5. deep _____

Dictionary Skills

A **syllable** is a part of a word that is pronounced at one time. Dictionary entry words are divided into syllables to show how they can be divided at the end of a writing line. A hyphen (-) is placed between syllables to separate them.
EXAMPLE: forest   for-est

Find each word in a dictionary. Then, write each word with a hyphen between each syllable.

1. crooked _____

2. shallow _____

3. panic _____

4. continue _____

5. cheerful _____

Word Wise

| panic | shallow | crooked | cheerful | continue |

Choose the word from the box that makes sense in the sentences below.

1. "Stay in the _____ part of

the pool where your feet can touch," said Mother.

2. Rob gave a _____ "hello"

as he walked past his teacher.

3. The hikers decided to _____ walking up the

trail when they finished lunch.

4. Kate had to slow down her bike because the path was so

_____.

5. Paco began to _____ when he couldn't find

his homework.

Writing

Write your own story about a time you went for a walk in a place that was new to you. Use as many of the vocabulary words from the box as you can.

_____

_____

_____

_____

_____

Name _____   Date _____

Apples, Apples, Apples

Read the story. Think about the meanings of the words in bold type.

Apples are **delicious**! They must be because we gobble up billions of them every year. There are many **varieties** of apples. Most people are **familiar** with red apples. But the apples that are green and yellow are not as well known. Some apples are very sweet. Others have a sharp, **tart** taste. Apples can be eaten fresh or **consumed** as yummy pies, applesauce, or apple juice. They are full of vitamins A and C. So eat some apples today! They are unbeatable for a tasty yet healthy treat.

Look back at the words in bold type. Use clues in the story to figure out the meaning of each word. Write each word on the line next to its meaning.

_____ **1.** eaten or drunk

_____ **2.** a sharp taste, almost sour

_____ **3.** know about

_____ **4.** pleasing to taste or smell

_____ **5.** different kinds

Unit 4, Lesson 19
Vocabulary Skills 3, SV 6902-7

Name _____ Date _____

Synonyms

Synonyms are words that have the same, or almost the same, meaning.
EXAMPLES: yell—shout   happy—glad   angry—mad

Match the words in the box with their synonyms. Write the words on the line.

> tart   consumed   familiar   delicious   varieties

1. yummy _____

2. eaten _____

3. sharp _____

4. known _____

5. kinds _____

Dictionary Skills

Guide words are at the top of each page in a dictionary. Guide words tell the first and last entry words listed on the page. Every word listed on the page comes between the guide words.

EXAMPLE: **tall**   **treat**
           tame, tea, teach, track

Darken the circle for the correct answer.

1. Which word would be between the guide words *talk* and *time*?
   Ⓐ treat   Ⓑ tart   Ⓒ tire   Ⓓ table

2. Which word would be between the guide words *dear* and *den*?
   Ⓐ depart   Ⓑ dented   Ⓒ dealer   Ⓓ delicious

3. Which word would be between the guide words *come* and *contain*?
   Ⓐ consumed   Ⓑ contest   Ⓒ comb   Ⓓ coach

Word Wise

tart   consumed   familiar   delicious   varieties

Choose the word from the box that makes sense in the sentences below.

1. The cookies Tom made were _____.

2. It was hard to choose just one kind of muffin when there were so many _____ from which to pick.

3. Ella was so hungry that she _____ the whole pizza by herself.

4. The _____ apple made Manuel frown when he took a big bite.

5. The new bus driver was not _____ with the route and did not know where to stop.

Writing

What kind of fruit do you like? Write your own story telling why you like it. Use as many of the vocabulary words from the box as you can.

_____

_____

_____

_____

_____

_____

Unit 5 Assessment, Page 2

Darken the letter of the correct answer.

9. Choose the suffix that means "full of."
   Ⓐ less
   Ⓑ ly
   Ⓒ ful
   Ⓓ ible

10. Choose the homophone that best completes the sentence.
    The cars had to _____ for the train to pass.
    Ⓐ wait
    Ⓑ wade
    Ⓒ weight
    Ⓓ whale

11. Which word comes from the Latin root *mot*, which means "move"?
    Ⓐ monster
    Ⓑ mother
    Ⓒ most
    Ⓓ motor

12. Choose the sentence in which the homophone *blew* or *blue* is used correctly.
    Ⓐ Sara bought a blue shirt.
    Ⓑ The wind blue the leaves off the tree.
    Ⓒ I like the blew shoes best.
    Ⓓ The blew boat is the fastest.

13. Which of the following suffixes can be added to the end of the word *fear* to make a new word?
    Ⓐ ly
    Ⓑ er
    Ⓒ able
    Ⓓ less

14. Which suffix changes the word *play* to mean "one who plays"?
    Ⓐ ful
    Ⓑ er
    Ⓒ ed
    Ⓓ less

15. Which word comes from the Spanish word *lazo*?
    Ⓐ lasso
    Ⓑ friend
    Ⓒ mesa
    Ⓓ mustang

16. Which is the root word of the word *beautiful*?
    Ⓐ beau
    Ⓑ ty
    Ⓒ beauty
    Ⓓ ful

Prefixes

A **prefix** is a syllable added to the beginning of a word
to change the meaning of the word.
EXAMPLES:
The prefix **un** means "not" or "the opposite of." **un**usual
The prefix **re** means "again" or "back." **re**heat

Complete each sentence by adding the prefix <u>un</u> or <u>re</u> to the word in ( ).

1. (able) Jan was _____ to go visit her friend.

2. (fair) She thought it was _____ that she had

to stay home.

3. (read) Jan decided to _____ her favorite

book.

4. (call) However, she could not _____ where

she left the book.

5. (like) It was _____ Jan to misplace

something.

6. (trace) Jan began to _____ her steps to find

the book.

7. (happy) She was very _____ when she could

not find the book.

8. (live) Jan hoped that she would never have to

_____ another day like this.

More Prefixes

Remember that a **prefix** is a syllable added to the beginning of a word to change the meaning of the word. The part of the word that the prefix is added to is called a **base** word or **root** word.

EXAMPLE: Julio is happy. Julio is **un**happy. (prefix = un; base word = happy)

Prefix	Meaning	Example
dis	not	dislike
im	not	impossible
re	again; back	return
un	not; opposite of	unwrap

Read each sentence. Change the meaning of each sentence by adding a prefix from the list above to each underlined word. Write the new word on the line.

1. Lexi was a very <u>usual</u> animal. _____

2. She was <u>patient</u> to get out into the world.

_____

3. Lexi <u>liked</u> the pet store. _____

4. Every night she felt <u>lucky</u> to be there. _____

5. Lexi thought it was <u>possible</u> to find a new home.

_____

6. Her hutch was <u>like</u> the cage at the pet store.

_____

7. A girl who looked at Lexi yesterday <u>appeared</u> today.

_____

8. Lexi was leaving the pet store and would never be <u>happy</u> again.

_____

Prefixes in Context

Choose a word from the box that makes sense in a sentence below. Use each word one time only.

return	unhappy	redo	impossible
unlike	reviewed	rewrite	

Mrs. Perez called Len to her desk. She told Len that it was

(1) _____ to read his homework. So Mrs. Perez

asked Len to (2) _____ the problems and

(3) _____ the homework the next day.

Len was (4) _____ that he had to

(5) _____ work, but he was surprised to find

several mistakes. It was (6) _____ him to miss

even one problem. Len was glad that he got to correct the homework. This

time, Len carefully (7) _____ each problem.

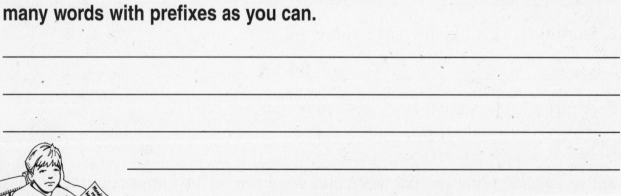

Writing

Write your own story about a time that you had to redo something. Use as many words with prefixes as you can.

_____

_____

_____

_____

_____

Suffixes

A **suffix** is a syllable added to the end of a word to change the meaning of the word.

EXAMPLES:

The suffix **ful** means "full of," "able to," or "the amount that will fill."
hope**ful**, help**ful**

The suffix **ly** means "in a certain way." quick**ly**, sudden**ly**

Complete each sentence by adding the suffix <u>ful</u> or <u>ly</u> to the word in ( ).

1. (bad) John's house needed a new coat of paint

_____ .

2. (friend) It was a hard job, so John asked a

_____ painter to do

the work.

3. (color) John asked the painter to choose a paint

that was bright and _____ .

4. (quick) The painter _____ began to work.

5. (quiet) She painted _____ for several days.

6. (care) The painter was very _____ not to

make a mess.

7. (wonder) When the painter was finished, John thought his house looked

_____ .

8. (happy) John _____ paid the painter.

More Suffixes

Remember that a **suffix** is a syllable added to the end of a word to change the meaning of the word or the way the word is used. The part of the word that the suffix is added to is called a **base** word or **root** word.

EXAMPLE: The child is quiet. The child played quiet**ly**.
(base word = quiet; suffix = ly)

Suffix	Meaning	Example
able	able to be	wear<u>able</u>
er	one who	sing<u>er</u>
ful	full of	help<u>ful</u>
ible	able to be	flex<u>ible</u>
less	without	care<u>less</u>
or	one who does	visit<u>or</u>

Read each sentence. Choose a suffix from the list above. Add it to the word in ( ). Then, write the word on the line. You may have to change the spelling.

1. Luke was an (person who invents) of many things. _____

2. One time Luke built a (able to work) roller coaster. _____

3. It was a (full of use) ride. _____

4. His sister Maxine was his (person who helps).

_____

5. Luke and Maxine were (without fear) and rode on it.

_____

6. They felt (full of joy) flying down the tracks.

_____

7. Their first (full of success) ride ended at their

grandmother's feet. _____

Suffixes in Context

Choose a word from the box that makes sense in a sentence below. Use each word one time only.

> leader   colorful   player   wonderful   loudly   happily   quickly

The school band was marching in a parade. It was a

(1) _____ sight. The members of the band wore

(2) _____ red and gold school uniforms. The

band (3) _____ marched in front to direct the

group. The flag guard smiled (4) _____ as they

twirled their flags. The band marched down the street and played the music

(5) _____ for everyone to hear. Three boys with

large drums were in the first row. Next came the people playing the horns

and trumpets. The tuba (6) _____ marched

behind. The smallest flute player was left behind and had to run

(7) _____ to catch up.

Writing

Write your own story about a parade you saw. Use as many words with suffixes as you can.

_____

_____

_____

_____

_____

Latin Roots

Many English words come from the same Latin root.
EXAMPLE: The Latin root *act* means "to do."
English words with the Latin root *act*: action, actor, react

Latin Root	Meaning
graph	write
mot	move
tract	pull, drag

Choose the word from the box that matches the meaning. Use the chart above to help you. Write the word on the line.

photograph	attract	tractor	motor
autograph	remote	subtract	motion

1. a machine that makes something work _____

2. a picture made with a camera _____

3. movement _____

4. to pull one thing away from another thing _____

5. a person's name written by that person _____

6. to cause to pull near _____

7. a vehicle used to pull heavy tools _____

8. moved far away from _____

Greek and Latin Roots

Many words in English come from Greek and Latin roots.

EXAMPLE: biography—a written history of a person's life from the Greek words **bios** meaning "life" and **graphein** meaning "to write"

Word	Meaning
metron	measure
bios	life
graphein	to write
tele	far away
hydra	water
skopein	look at
centum	hundred
mikros	small

Write the word from the box that matches the meaning.

telegraph	telescope	centimeter
micrometer	hydroscope	microscope

1. This allows you to write to people far away.

_____

2. This allows you to look at something that is very small.

_____

3. This allows you to look at something under water.

_____

4. This is a unit of measurement that is $\frac{1}{100}$ of a meter.

_____

5. This allows you to look at something far away.

_____

6. This is a tool that lets you measure small distances.

_____

Prefixes, Suffixes, and Root Words

Many English words are made of a combination of prefixes, suffixes, and root words. Knowing the meanings of the different parts of a word can help you find the meaning of the word.

EXAMPLE: reactor = one who does something again

prefix **re** = again

root **act** = to do

suffix **or** = one who

Prefix	Meaning
im	within, into
im	not
in	into
un	not

Root	Meaning
aequalis	like
imaginare	to picture in one's mind
patiens	to endure
portare	to carry
quietus	freedom from noise
segregare	to separate

Suffix	Meaning
able	can do or can be done
er, or	one who
ion	state, quality
ly	in the manner of
tion	the state of

Use the charts to write the meanings of the words.

1. quietly _____

2. porter _____

3. imagination _____

4. unequal _____

5. impatient _____

6. inseparable _____

Homophones

Homophones are words that sound the same but have different meanings and usually different spellings.

EXAMPLES: to, too, two   their, there, and they're

To means "in the direction of." Lets go **to** the mountains.

Too means "also." John will be going, **too**.

Two means "one more than one." Meg has **two** dogs.

Their means "belonging to them." That is **their** house.

There means "in or at that place." Put it **there**.

They're means "they are." **They're** going to the game.

Read each sentence. Choose and circle the correct word in ( ).

1. Let's go (to, too) the park.

2. We will see other friends in the park, (two, too).

3. Jim and Alex said they will be (their, there).

4. (There, They're) going to get to the park before noon.

5. Did they say they would bring (they're, their) bats?

6. (Their, There) is a place to play baseball.

7. If we took our (two, to) balls, we could practice batting.

8. We can't forget (two, to) take our lunch.

More Homophones

Remember that **homophones** are words that sound the same but have different meanings and usually different spellings.
EXAMPLES: to, two, too   hear, here

Read each pair of words in ( ). Then, complete each sentence by writing each word from the pair where it makes sense.

1. (hear, here) Did I _____ that the circus is

coming _____ next week?

2. (blue, blew) The wind _____ the

_____ sailboat across the ocean.

3. (scene, seen) I have never _____ a more

beautiful _____ than those mountains.

4. (ate, eight) He always _____ breakfast at

_____ o'clock.

5. (our, hour) At what _____ will

_____ grandmother arrive?

6. (one, won) That author _____ an award for

_____ of her books.

7. (ant, aunt) Jay's _____ got bitten on her

finger by an _____.

8. (four, for) The _____ children did not know

what to eat _____ lunch.

Reading and Writing Homophones

Remember that **homophones** are words that sound the same but have different meanings and usually different spellings.

EXAMPLE: **Rode** means "sat on or in something to be carried."
Road means "a path used to go from one place to another."
The cowboy **rode** down the **road**.

Look at each pair of homophones. Then use both homophones in a sentence. Draw a picture to go with each sentence.

1. see, sea

_____

_____

2. write, right

_____

_____

3. blew, blue

_____

_____

4. wood, would

_____

_____

Words from Spanish

Many English words come from other languages. One language is Spanish.
EXAMPLE: rodeo   The most exciting part of the **rodeo** is bullriding.

Write the English word that comes from each Spanish word.

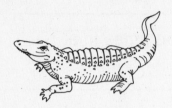

1. This word comes from the Spanish *lagarto*.

_____

2. This word comes from the Spanish *patata*.

_____

3. This word comes from the Spanish *mesa*.

_____

4. This word comes from the Spanish *mosca*.

_____

5. This word comes from the Spanish *lazo*.

_____

6. This word comes from the Spanish *mesteño*.

_____

Clothing Words from Other Languages

The girl below is wearing clothing from different parts of the world. Read the list of clothing names that come from other languages. Then, fill in the labels on the picture.

Clothing	Description	Origin
bandana	square of cloth	India
beret	small, flat hat	France
bolero	short vest	Spain
kimono	robe	Japan
moccasin	soft leather shoe	United States (Native American)
parka	hooded coat	Russia
skirt	covering that hangs from the waist	Scandinavia
sombrero	hat with wide brim	Spain
tote	carrying bag	Africa

More Words from Other Languages

Many words we use in English come from countries and cultures all around the world.

> **alfresco**—an Italian word meaning "outdoors"
> **bon voyage**—French words meaning "have a good trip"
> **clan**—a Scottish word meaning "family"
> **mesas**—a Spanish word meaning "flat-topped hills"
> **mustangs**—from a Spanish word meaning "wild horses"
> **raccoon**—from an Algonquian Native American word meaning "he who scratches with his hands"

Use the words in bold type above to complete the story.

The whole Jones (1) _____

loves to travel. They go to many faraway places.

They have had (2) _____

picnics in the Alp Mountains. They

have climbed flat-topped

(3) _____

in Mexico. The Jones family especially loves

to watch animals. They have seen wild (4) _____

racing across the plains. They have watched a furry

(5) _____ washing its meal in a stream.

Soon, they are going on another interesting trip. They will be saying

"(6) _____" as they wave good-bye.

Fun with Context Clues

Read the sentences. Use context clues to decide what the words in dark print would mean if they were real words. Then, explain why your meanings make sense.

1. Roger helped his dad plant a **glonock**.

   meaning: _____

   explanation: _____

2. He used a **tryglif** to dig the hole.

   meaning: _____

   explanation: _____

3. Then, Roger's dad put the plant in the hole and pushed the extra **vim** around the trunk.

   meaning: _____

   explanation: _____

4. Finally, Roger gave the plant some **flizzen** with a hose.

   meaning: _____

   explanation: _____

Fun with Homograph Riddles

Homographs are words that have the same spelling but different meanings. Sometimes homographs have different pronunciations.
EXAMPLE: Two **live** monkeys **live** with Ken.

Read each riddle. Tell what the underlined word means in each riddle. Then, write a sentence to show a different meaning for each underlined word.

1. Question: When is a piece of wood like a king?
   Answer: when it's a <u>ruler</u>

   meaning: _____

   sentence: _____

2. Question: Why do watermelons have water in them?
   Answer: because they are planted in the <u>spring</u>

   meaning: _____

   sentence: _____

3. Question: Why did the farmer call his pig Ink?
   Answer: because it kept running out of the <u>pen</u>

   meaning: _____

   sentence: _____

Vocabulary Skills, Grade 3, Answer Key

pages 4–5
1. C, **2.** B, **3.** C, **4.** A, **5.** D,
6. D, **7.** A, **8.** D, **9.** A, **10.** B,
11. C, **12.** C, **13.** A, **14.** C,
15. C, **16.** A, **17.** A, **18.** D

pages 6–7
1. B, **2.** C, **3.** A, **4.** B, **5.** D,
6. C, **7.** A, **8.** D, **9.** A, **10.** B,
11. C, **12.** A, **13.** D, **14.** B,
15. D, **16.** A, **17.** B, **18.** C

pages 8–9
1. C, **2.** B, **3.** A, **4.** C, **5.** A,
6. D, **7.** C, **8.** A, **9.** B, **10.** D,
11. B, **12.** D, **13.** B, **14.** C,
15. C, **16.** A, **17.** D, **18.** A,
19. C, **20.** B

page 10
1. timid, **2.** bored, **3.** cautious,
4. dull, **5.** brave

page 11
Antonyms:
1. brave, **2.** timid, **3.** bored,
4. dull, **5.** cautious
Dictionary Skills:
1. bored, **2.** brave, **3.** cautious,
4. dull, **5.** timid

page 12
1. cautious, **2.** timid, **3.** brave,
4. bored, **5.** dull

page 13
1. tear, **2.** scratch, **3.** wound,
4. lead, **5.** leash

page 14
1. B, **2.** A, **3.** B, **4.** A, **5.** A, **6.** B

page 15
Sentences may vary.
1. Mother does not like it when
we tear around the house.
2. The old dog began to
scratch its ear.
3. When the children lined up,
Myra was in the lead.
4. Fred wound a rope swing
around the tree branch.
5. John always walks his dog
on a leash.

page 16
1. equal, **2.** breeds, **3.** massive,
4. petite, **5.** enjoy

page 17
Synonyms:
1. E, **2.** C, **3.** A, **4.** B, **5.** D
Dictionary Skills:
1. C, **2.** B, **3.** A

page 18
1. breeds, **2.** petite, **3.** massive,
4. equal, **5.** enjoy

page 19
1. damage, **2.** sore, **3.** ankle,
4. thud, **5.** pursuing

page 20
Word Groups:
1. damage, **2.** ankle, **3.** sore,
4. thud, **5.** pursuing
Dictionary Skills:
Answers may vary depending
on the dictionary used.
1. thud, **2.** pur-su-ing, **3.** sore,
4. dam-age, **5.** an-kle

page 21
1. thud, **2.** ankle, **3.** pursuing,
4. damage, **5.** sore

page 22
1. felines, **2.** unbelievable,
3. peaceful, **4.** frisky, **5.** cleanse

page 23
1. felines, **2.** cleanse, **3.** frisky,
4. unbelievable, **5.** peaceful

page 24
Sentences may vary.
1. Gina's horse could do tricks
that were unbelievable.
2. The frisky puppy raced
around the yard.
3. Many felines like to be left
alone.
4. Sue found the park peaceful
after a visit to the noisy city.
5. The nurse had to cleanse the
dirt from Rachel's eye.

pages 25–26
1. A, **2.** C, **3.** B, **4.** A, **5.** C,
6. B, **7.** A, **8.** B, **9.** D, **10.** A,
11. D, **12.** A, **13.** C, **14.** B,
15. B, **16.** A, **17.** D, **18.** C,
19. A, **20.** C

page 27
1. crafty, **2.** embraced,
3. discovered, **4.** sneaking,
5. disguised

page 28
Sentences will vary.
1. embrace, **2.** craft,
3. discover, **4.** sneak,
5. disguise

page 29
Sentences may vary.
1. Tim was sneaking close to
the birds so he would not scare
them away.
2. Marie discovered that her
computer had a bug.
3. That crafty fish just took my
bait!
4. Matt disguised himself so
that he could spy on his sister.
5. Mrs. Hugo embraced her
son when he got home from
school.

page 30
1. gift, **2.** rare, **3.** silk,
4. emperor, **5.** received

page 31
Analogies:
1. rare, **2.** emperor, **3.** gift,
4. silk, **5.** received
Dictionary Skills:
1. emperor, **2.** gift, **3.** rare,
4. received, **5.** silk

page 32
1. rare, **2.** silk, **3.** emperor,
4. received, **5.** gift

page 33
1. foolish, **2.** solve, **3.** clues,
4. burglar, **5.** haste

page 34
Synonyms:
1. haste, **2.** clues, **3.** foolish,
4. burglar, **5.** solve
Dictionary Skills:
1. burglar, **2.** clues, **3.** foolish,
4. haste, **5.** solve

page 35
1. clues, **2.** burglar, **3.** foolish,
4. haste, **5.** solve

page 36
1. character, **2.** usually,
3. swift, **4.** errors, **5.** legends

page 37
Word Groups:
1. character, **2.** legends,
3. errors, **4.** swift, **5.** usually
Dictionary Skills:
1. A, **2.** C, **3.** D

page 38
1. usually, **2.** character,
3. swift, **4.** legends, **5.** errors

page 39
1. business, **2.** make-believe,
3. various, **4.** imagination,
5. exciting

page 40
1. make-believe,
2. imagination, **3.** exciting,
4. business, **5.** various

page 41
1. various, **2.** exciting,
3. make-believe, **4.** business,
5. imagination

pages 42–43
1. B, **2.** D, **3.** A, **4.** A, **5.** B,
6. D, **7.** C, **8.** A, **9.** B, **10.** D,
11. C, **12.** A, **13.** D, **14.** A,
15. C, **16.** D, **17.** B, **18.** A,
19. C, **20.** D

page 44
1. baseball, **2.** airport,
3. homework, **4.** hallway,
5. classroom

page 45
Answer order may vary.
1. airport, **2.** classroom,
3. hallway, **4.** baseball,
5. homework

page 46
Sentences may vary.
1. The teacher turned on the
lights in the classroom.
2. Mr. Ruiz gave us ten math
problems for homework.
3. We drove to the airport to
pick up my grandmother.
4. Larry and his friends went
to the park to play baseball.
5. The children walked quietly
in the hallway.

page 47
1. exercise, **2.** frigid,
3. supermarket, **4.** tramp,
5. perspiration

page 48
Synonyms:
1. exercise, **2.** frigid,
3. supermarket, **4.** perspiration,
5. tramp
Dictionary Skills:
Answers may vary depending
on the dictionary used.
1. ex-er-cise, **2.** tramp,
3. frig-id, **4.** per-spi-ra-tion,
5. su-per-mar-ket

page 49
1. perspiration, **2.** frigid,
3. tramp, **4.** supermarket,
5. exercise

page 50
1. astonished, **2.** childhood,
3. homesick, **4.** seacoast,
5. reminded

page 51
Across
1. reminded, **2.** homesick,
3. childhood
Down
4. seacoast, **5.** astonished

page 52
Sentences will vary.

page 53
1. content, **2.** dove, **3.** amazed,
4. bent, **5.** palm

page 54
1. A, **2.** B, **3.** B, **4.** A, **5.** B,
6. A

page 55
1. bent, **2.** amazed, **3.** content,
4. dove, **5.** palm

page 56
1. grumpy, **2.** outdoorsmen,
3. canoe, **4.** poncho,
5. compass

page 57
1. compass, 2. canoe,
3. grumpy, 4. outdoorsmen,
5. poncho

page 58
Sentences may vary.
1. Anna and her dad were outdoorsmen and spent time hiking through the woods each weekend.
2. The ship's captain used a compass when the storm blew them off course.
3. Soon Lei tried to cheer up Jake when she saw that he was grumpy.
4. Many people who go to baseball games take a poncho.
5. Grandpa said that he would take me for a ride in the canoe after lunch.

pages 59–60
1. D, 2. A, 3. C, 4. A, 5. B,
6. D, 7. C, 8. C, 9. A, 10. B,
11. D, 12. C, 13. A, 14. D,
15. A, 16. D, 17. B, 18. A,
19. D, 20. B

page 61
1. universe, 2. surface,
3. molten, 4. orbits, 5. depths

page 62
Sentences will vary.
1. orbits, 2. universe,
3. surface, 4. depths, 5. molten
Answer: It is a star.

page 63
1. orbits, 2. depths, 3. universe,
4. surface, 5. molten

page 64
1. electricity, 2. lightning,
3. flashlight, 4. frightened,
5. thunder

page 65
Answers will vary.

page 66
Sentences may vary.
1. Glen saw lightning flash across the sky.
2. Then, he heard the thunder that followed.
3. Glen wondered if the electricity would go off so there would be no lights.
4. He went to look for a flashlight.
5. The light would keep him from feeling frightened.

page 67
1. panic, 2. cheerful,
3. continue, 4. crooked,
5. shallow

page 68
Antonyms:
1. crooked, 2. panic,
3. cheerful, 4. continue,
5. shallow
Dictionary Skills:
Answers may vary depending on the dictionary used.
1. crook-ed, 2. shal-low,
3. pan-ic, 4. con-tin-ue,
5. cheer-ful

page 69
1. shallow, 2. cheerful,
3. continue, 4. crooked,
5. panic

page 70
1. consumed, 2. tart,
3. familiar, 4. delicious,
5. varieties

page 71
Synonyms:
1. delicious, 2. consumed,
3. tart, 4. familiar, 5. varieties
Dictionary Skills:
1. B, 2. D, 3. A

page 72
1. delicious, 2. varieties,
3. consumed, 4. tart, 5. familiar

page 73
1. cycles, 2. nutrients,
3. ecosystem, 4. fuel,
5. smoldered

page 74
1. smoldered, 2. nutrients,
3. cycles, 4. ecosystem, 5. fuel

page 75
Sentences may vary.
1. Grandpa talks about the cycles on the farm, like the growing of crops.
2. Coal used to be fuel in factories many years ago.
3. Rabbits and trees are an important part of the forest ecosystem.
4. People need many nutrients to help keep them strong and healthy.
5. The house smoldered for several days after the firefighters put out the fire.

pages 76–77
1. B, 2. A, 3. C, 4. D, 5. D,
6. B, 7. B, 8. C, 9. C, 10. A,
11. D, 12. A, 13. D, 14. B,
15. A, 16. C

page 78
1. unable, 2. unfair, 3. reread,
4. recall, 5. unlike, 6. retrace,
7. unhappy, 8. relive

page 79
1. unusual, 2. impatient,
3. disliked, 4. unlucky,
5. impossible, 6. unlike,
7. reappeared, 8. unhappy

page 80
1. impossible, 2. rewrite or redo, 3. return, 4. unhappy,
5. redo or rewrite, 6. unlike,
7. reviewed

page 81
1. badly, 2. friendly,
3. colorful, 4. quickly,
5. quietly, 6. careful,
7. wonderful, 8. happily

page 82
1. inventor, 2. workable,
3. useful, 4. helper, 5. fearless,
6. joyful, 7. successful

page 83
1. wonderful, 2. colorful,
3. leader, 4. happily, 5. loudly,
6. player, 7. quickly

page 84
1. motor, 2. photograph,
3. motion, 4. subtract,
5. autograph, 6. attract,
7. tractor, 8. remote

page 85
1. telegraph, 2. microscope,
3. hydroscope, 4. centimeter,
5. telescope, 6. micrometer

page 86
Definitions may vary.
1. done in a manner that is free from noise, 2. one who carries,
3. the state of picturing in one's mind, 4. not alike,
5. not able to endure,
6. not able to separate

page 87
1. to, 2. too, 3. there,
4. They're, 5. their, 6. There,
7. two, 8. to

page 88
1. hear; here, 2. blew; blue,
3. seen; scene, 4. ate; eight,
5. hour; our, 6. won; one,
7. aunt; ant, 8. four; for

page 89
Sentences will vary.

page 90
1. alligator, 2. potato,
3. mesa, 4. mosquito, 5. lasso,
6. mustang

page 91
beret—hat; bandana—bandana;
bolero—vest; kimono—dress;
skirt—skirt; tote—purse;
moccasins—shoes

page 92
1. clan, 2. alfresco, 3. mesas,
4. mustangs, 5. raccoon,
6. bon voyage

page 93
Answers will vary.

page 94
Answers will vary.
1. underlined meaning: a measuring tool; another meaning: a ruler of a country,
2. underlined meaning: a season of the year; another meaning: water that comes up from the ground, 3. underlined meaning: a place to keep animals; another meaning: a writing tool